TIMELINES
OF ANCIENT CIVILIZATIONS

CHINA

David and Patricia Armentrout

Rourke
Publishing LLC
Vero Beach, Florida 32964

www.rourkepublishing.com

PHOTO CREDITS: © Al Michaud pgs 10, 18, 24, 26; © Jurgen Ankenbrand Cover, pg 12; © Corel Corporation Title, pg 16; © Hulton/Archive by Getty Images pgs 14, 20, 23 © Painet, Inc. pg 7; © University of Missouri-Columbia/Daniel S. Glover pg 8; © Map by Artville

Title page: *The Chinese people are proud of their country's collection of ancient art.*

Editor: Frank Sloan

Cover and interior design by Nicola Stratford

Library of Congress Cataloging-in-Publication Data

Armentrout, David, 1962-
    China / David and Patricia Armentrout.
        v. cm. — (Timelines of ancient civilizations)
Includes index.
Contents: 2202-AD 1911 An ancient civilization — 2205-1600 BC Hsia Dynasty — 1600-1027 BC Shang Dynasty — 1027-221 BC Zhou Dynasty and warring states -- 221-206 BC Qin Dynasty -- 206 BC-AD 220 Han Dynasty — AD 220-589 Period of disunity — AD 589-906 Sui and Tang Dynasties — AD 960-1279 Song Dynasty — AD 1279-1368 Yuan Dynasty — AD 1368-1644 Ming Dynasty — AD 1644-1911 Qing Dynasty.
    ISBN 1-58952-719-4 (hardcover)
    1. China—Civilization—Chronology—Juvenile literature. [1. China—Civilization—Chronology.] I. Armentrout, Patricia, 1960- II. Title. II. Series: Armentrout, David, 1962- Timelines of ancient civilizations.
    DS721.A696 2003
    951'.002'02—dc21
                                                            2003001757

Printed in the USA

CG/CG

CONTENTS

2205 BC-AD 1911 An Ancient Civilization 4

2205-1600 BC Hsia Dynasty 6

1600-1027 BC Shang Dynasty 8

1027-221 BC Zhou Dynasty and
Warring States 10

221-206 BC Qin Dynasty 12

206 BC-AD 220 Han Dynasty 14

AD 220-589 Period of Disunity 16

AD 589-906 Sui and Tang Dynasties 18

AD 960-1279 Song Dynasty 20

AD 1279-1368 Yuan Dynasty 22

AD 1368-1644 Ming Dynasty 24

AD 1644-1911 Qing Dynasty 26

Timeline 28

Glossary 30

Pronunciation Guide 31

Further Reading/Websites to Visit 31

Index 32

2205 BC-AD 1911

AN ANCIENT CIVILIZATION

China is a huge country located in east Asia. Today it is the third largest nation in the world and has a population of more than one billion people. There is no doubt that China is also one of the world's oldest **civilizations**. A civilization is a human society that is organized. A civilization usually has a written language and is highly developed in the arts and sciences.

Ruling families, or groups, known as **dynasties** controlled ancient China. Dynasties sometimes lasted for hundreds of years.

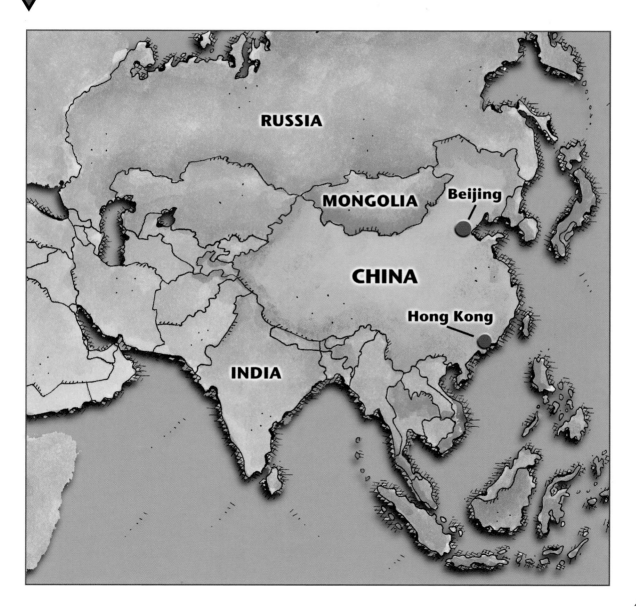

RUSSIA

MONGOLIA   Beijing

CHINA

Hong Kong

INDIA

2205-1600 BC

HSIA DYNASTY

Historians believe the first Chinese dynasty, known as the Hsia, came to power in the 23rd century BC. The Hsia dynasty ruled over the Longshan people.

Archaeologists discovered **artifacts** that belonged to the Longshan. The artifacts show that the Longshan were advanced for their time. They farmed their land, wove silk fabric, and made pottery containers. The Hsia dynasty lost control of China around 1600 BC. They were replaced by a new family called the Shang.

2205 BC–AD 1911

2205–1600 BC

1600–1027 BC

1027–221 BC

221–206 BC

206 BC–AD 220

AD 220–589

AD 589–906

AD 960–1279

AD 1279–1368

AD 1368–1644

AD 1644–1911

The Chinese learned to grow food thousands of years ago.

7

1600-1027 BC

SHANG DYNASTY

A written language was developed during the Shang dynasty. The first examples of early Chinese writing were found on engraved animal bones called oracle bones.

No other civilization has surpassed the Shang's skill with bronze metal work. They made beautiful bronze vessels.

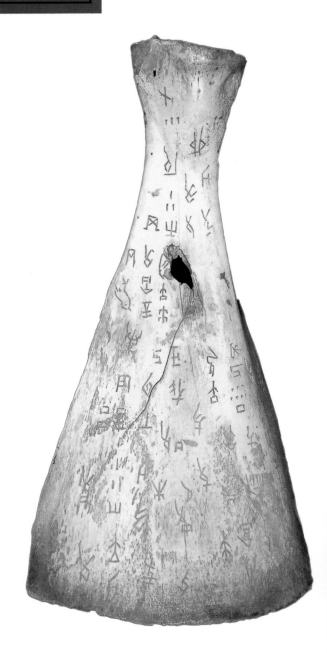

Shoulder bones of cattle or water buffalo were often used for engraving.

They also used bronze to make weapons of war. Horses pulled chariots made with wood and bronze. Warriors dressed in bronze armor rode in these chariots and swung bronze axes and daggers at their enemies.

Thousands of oracle bones have been found in China. The Shang engraved questions on the bones. The bones were then scorched with hot metal. Fortune tellers answered the questions by "reading" cracks that appeared.

1027-221 BC

ZHOU DYNASTY AND WARRING STATES

The Shang were conquered by the Zhou in about 1027 BC. The Zhou lasted longer than any other dynasty in Chinese history. The early years of the Zhou dynasty were peaceful. As time went on, though, Zhou kings began to lose power to landowners and warlords.

This shift in power led to the "Warring States" period. Huge armies headed by warlords fought terrible battles. Millions died.

The Zhou period was violent, but it was also a time of great change. Inventions, such as iron farm tools and **irrigation** systems, made farms more productive. More food led to great increases in population.

Although he lived thousands of years ago, the teachings of Confucius are still very popular.

Confucius was a teacher who lived during the Zhou dynasty. Confucius believed rulers should lead with kindness and respect. Confucius was known for many famous sayings. One of them goes like this: "Do not do to others what you do not want them to do to you."

11

221-206 BC

QIN DYNASTY

The Qin dynasty took control of the warring states in about 221 BC. The Qin dynasty did not last long, but it left its mark on history. The Qin king wanted to protect his territory. He ordered that a huge wall be built to keep invaders out.

Hundreds of thousands of laborers were used to connect a series of existing smaller walls. Later dynasties would rebuild the wall and add to its length. The Great Wall would eventually be more than 1,500 miles (2,414 kilometers) long. Today, it is one of China's most popular tourist attractions.

Archaeologists discovered an amazing site near the tomb of the Qin emperor Shi Huangdi. An army of life-sized terra cotta (clay) soldiers, chariots, servants, and horses was buried next to the emperor's tomb.

Chinese archaeologists have spent years uncovering the terra cotta army.

HAN DYNASTY

The Qin dynasty ruled harshly. High taxes and unfair laws led to a **peasant** revolt. The next dynasty to rule China would be the Han.

The Han dynasty is known for its advances in technology. A Han official invented the first true paper, hundreds of years before it was invented elsewhere. It was made from plant fiber and silk rags. The raw materials were softened in water, boiled, and then pressed on a screen. When dry, a sheet of coarse paper was peeled off the screen.

The papermaking process was time consuming and expensive.

The Chinese have long been known for their beautiful pottery and ceramics. Porcelain, a type of fine ceramic, was invented during the Han dynasty.

AD 220-589

PERIOD OF DISUNITY

The period of disunity was a time of unrest in China. The empire was split into states and ruled by a number of different dynasties.

The ancient Chinese carved this Buddha into the side of a cliff. The entire carving is 231 feet (70.4 meters) tall.

The Buddhist religion spread throughout China during this period. Peaceful Buddhist teachings became popular in Chinese society.

A lasting invention of this period is the wheelbarrow. It may not seem like such a major invention, but it allowed a single person to move heavy loads. Wheelbarrows are still used almost everywhere in the world.

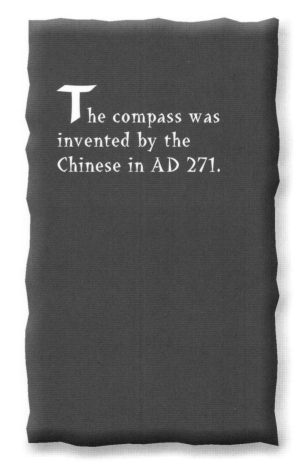

The compass was invented by the Chinese in AD 271.

AD 589-906

SUI AND TANG DYNASTIES

The Sui dynasty united China's separate states in AD 589. In the Sui's short rule, they rebuilt the Great Wall and started construction of the Grand Canal. The canal is hundreds of miles long and connects two major rivers.

The Sui soon gave way to the Tang dynasty. The Tang ruled for the next three hundred years. Under Tang rule, China became one of the largest and wealthiest empires on Earth.

The Tang used **engraved** wood blocks to create the world's first printed book. The book was a Buddhist textbook called the Diamond Sutra.

Gunpowder was probably invented in China. Although no one knows exactly when, many historians believe it was first discovered during the Tang dynasty. The Chinese may also have been the first to use gunpowder to make fireworks.

The Great Wall helped keep invaders out, but it also kept the Chinese people separated from the rest of the world.

AD 960-1279

SONG DYNASTY

The Song dynasty was a time of peace. Cities grew large and trade became more important than ever. Improved rice growing methods and **distribution** led to a booming population.

Tai Tsu was the first emperor of the Song dynasty.

Historians estimate that 100 million people may have lived in China by the early 12th century.

Printing, invented by the Tang, became much more common during the Song dynasty. The use of faster and cheaper printing methods meant that more people could afford books and a higher education.

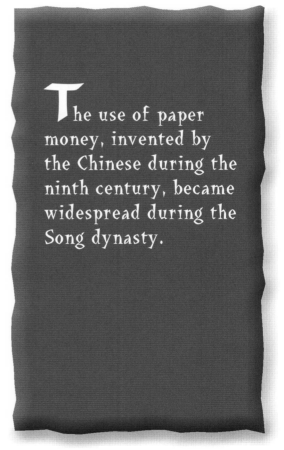

The use of paper money, invented by the Chinese during the ninth century, became widespread during the Song dynasty.

AD 1279-1368

YUAN DYNASTY

The Mongols invaded China during the 13th century AD. A famous warrior named Genghis Khan ruled the Mongols.

Ruthless Mongol armies conquered northern sections of China by about 1215. Several decades later, Kublai Khan, grandson of Genghis Khan, succeeded in taking control of the rest of China. Kublai Khan founded the Yuan dynasty in AD 1279. The Mongols ruled most of China until 1368.

Marco Polo was an Italian explorer. He became one of the first Europeans to travel through much of China. He was hired by Kublai Khan to represent the emperor on missions throughout China.

Marco Polo wrote a book about his travels in China.

23

AD 1368-1644

MING DYNASTY

Less than one hundred years after being conquered by the Mongols, the Chinese regained power. The Mongols were driven out and replaced by the Ming dynasty. The Ming dynasty ruled China for nearly three hundred years.

During the Ming dynasty, China sent a fleet of ships to explore the Indian Ocean. Mongol Admiral Zheng He commanded the fleet. Zheng He visited foreign rulers on behalf of the Chinese. During one of his expeditions, Zheng He's fleet sailed all the way to the east coast of Africa.

The Ming dynasty is known for its beautiful porcelain. Ming porcelain became a major trade product with Europeans.

The Ming tombs in China contain the remains of Ming dynasty emperors. The tomb of Emperor WanLi is reached by descending a long series of staircases.

AD 1644-1911

QING DYNASTY

The Manchu people from Manchuria conquered China in 1644. The Manchu set up the Qing dynasty. During the early part of the Qing dynasty the Chinese empire grew to include more territory than ever before.

2205 BC–AD 1911
2205–1600 BC
1600–1027 BC
1027–221 BC
221–206 BC
206 BC–AD 220
AD 220–589
AD 589–906
AD 960–1279
AD 1279–1368
AD 1368–1644
AD 1644–1911

By the 19th century, the Qing dynasty began to lose control. Trade conflicts led to war with the British. In 1898 China agreed to give up control of Hong Kong Island. In the agreement, China was forced to lease Hong Kong to the British for 99 years.

In 1911, revolution broke out. The Qing dynasty came to an end. The new government formed the first Chinese **Republic**, ending thousands of years of dynasties.

The magnificent Puning Temple was built during the Qing dynasty.

Timeline

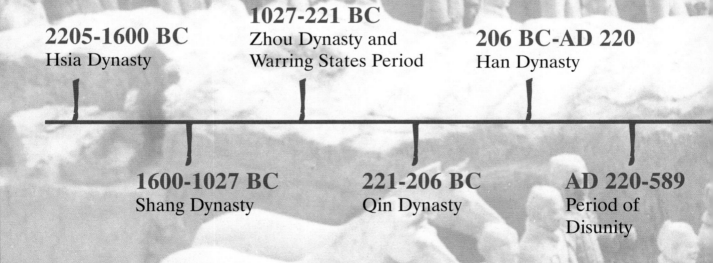

2205-1600 BC
Hsia Dynasty

1027-221 BC
Zhou Dynasty and
Warring States Period

206 BC-AD 220
Han Dynasty

1600-1027 BC
Shang Dynasty

221-206 BC
Qin Dynasty

AD 220-589
Period of
Disunity

AD 589-906
Sui and Tang
Dynasty

AD 1279-1368
Yuan Dynasty

AD 1644-1911
Qing Dynasty

AD 960-1279
Song Dynasty

AD 1368-1644
Ming Dynasty

29

GLOSSARY

archaeologists (AR kee AHL uh jests) — people who study past human life by examining artifacts left by ancient people

artifacts (ART eh fakts) — objects made or changed by humans

civilizations (siv eh leh ZAY shunz) — advanced levels of cultural development

distribution (diss tri BYOO shun) — the way things are divided over an area

dynasties (DYE nuh steez) — a series of rulers belonging to the same family or group

engraved (en GRAYVED) — signs or letters cut into an object's surface

irrigation (ir uh GAY shun) — to supply water to crops by using channels or pipes

peasant (PEZ uhnt) — a small farm owner, or someone who works on a farm

republic (ree PUB lik) — a government in which the people have the power to elect their representatives

PRONUNCIATION GUIDE

Hsia (SHYAH)
Qin (CHIN)
Quing (CHING)
Sui (SWAY)
Yuan (yoo AHN)
Zhou (JOH)

FURTHER READING

Cotterell, Arthur. *Ancient China.* Alfred A. Knopf 1994

O'Connor, Jane. *The Emperor's Silent Army.* Viking
    Children's Books 2002

Rees, Rosemary. *The Ancient Chinese.* Heinemann Library
    2002

WEBSITES TO VISIT

www.kidskonnect.com/

emuseum.mnsu.edu/prehistory/china/index.html

INDEX

bronze   8, 9

Great Wall   12, 13, 18

Han   14, 15

Hong Kong   27

Hsia   6

Marco Polo   23

Ming   24, 25

Mongols   22

oracle bones   8

paper   15

paper money   21

porcelain   15, 25

Qin   12

Qing   26, 27

Shang   6, 8, 10

Song   20, 21

Sui   18, 19

Tang   19

wheelbarrow   17

Yuan   22

Zhou   10, 11

ABOUT THE AUTHORS

David and Patricia Armentrout have written many nonfiction books for young readers. They have had several books published for primary school reading. The Armentrouts live in Cincinnati, Ohio, with their two children.